UNION SOLDIER
of the American
CIVIL WAR

Denis Hambucken
Chris Benedetto

ACKNOWLEDGMENTS

Many thanks to the individuals and organizations that have shared
their time, knowledge, and passion with us. This book could not
have been constructed without their help.

Kermit Hummel
Matt Payson
Christopher Reiter
Dr. Michael Echols
Special thanks to the 5th New Hampshire Volunteer Regiment

Photographs, illustrations, book design and composition
by Denis Hambucken
Editing by Lisa Sacks
Historic typefaces by Walden Fonts

Library of Congress Cataloging-in-Publication Data have been applied for.
Union soldier of the American Civil War
978-0-88150-971-7

Published by The Countryman Press, P.O. Box 748, Woodstock, VT 05091
Distributed by W. W. Norton & Company, Inc., 500 Fifth Avenue, New York, NY 10110

Printed in the United States of America
10 9 8 7 6 5 4 3 2 1

COLONEL RUSH'S
LIGHT CAVALRY.

NO COMPROMISE WITH TRAITORS, and No Argument but the Cannon's Mouth.

Company K,
ACTIVE MEN WANTED!

THE REGIMENT IS NOW IN CAMP ON THE

Second Street Road ab. Nicetown Lane.

This Company will be fully Equipped here, with

HORSES, ARMS, AND CLOTHING.

RECRUITING STATION

403 Chestnut Street.

T. W. NEILL, 1st Lieut. 2d "   HOWARD ELLIS, Captain.

KING & BAIRD, Printers No. 607 Sansom Street, Philadelphia.

CONTENTS

THE SITUATION IN OHIO.

LITTLE BUCKEYE. "Daddy, Old Secesh's coming across, sure.
DADDY. "All right, Sonny! but I've ben' waiting a blessed long time for him."

THE LIFE & TIMES
OF THE UNION SOLDIER

THE LIFE & TIMES OF THE UNION SOLDIER

Prior to the inauguration of President Abraham Lincoln, seven Southern states had seceded from the United States, forming the Confederate States of America. On April 12, 1861, the Confederacy fired the opening volley of the American Civil War as it bombarded Fort Sumter to evict Federal troops from Charleston Harbor.

On April 15, 1861, only one day after the surrender of Fort Sumter, Lincoln issued a call for 75,000 volunteers to quell the "great rebellion." With a single stroke of his pen, he quadrupled the size of the U.S. Army, thus creating an American military force of unprecedented size and firepower

His subsequent calls to service, over the four-year course of the war, drew nearly 3 million men into the Union ranks. While the first 75,000 volunteer troops enlisted for only ninety days, the remaining volunteers signed up for three years, or the duration of the war. Among the Union soldiers were nearly 200,000 African American men, many of them former slaves, who were eager to prove their worth and to defeat slavery forever.

For many men, the call of duty and patriotism was far too strong to resist. Darius K. Scruton left his wife, Harriet, and five children behind in Rollinsford, New Hampshire, in the autumn of 1861. He was deployed to South Carolina with the 3rd New Hampshire Volunteer Infantry Regiment.

After he was seriously wounded in June 1862, Lieutenant Scruton returned home and died in August after refusing to allow the local doctor to amputate his arm. In many ways, Scruton's tragic story is representative of the fate that all too many men suffered in the war.

Unlike many of their Yankee ancestors who perhaps fought during the Revolution and drilled with their local militia, the vast majority of volunteers had little familiarity with military protocol. Many others were recent immigrants from Ireland or Germany who came to work in the mills of New England or settle in the fertile farmland of Pennsylvania and the Midwest. Whether they saw a recruiting broadside posted at the local mill, attended a patriotic rally, or were recruited by an aspiring officer, the way they enlisted was essentially the same. Volunteers reported to a recruiting station where they had to pass a dubious medical exam. Per army regulations, the minimum age for enlistment was eighteen, and recruits under the age of twenty-one needed the consent of a parent. However, many teenage boys lied

Many newly enlisted men proudly sent home photos of themselves in their fresh uniforms. The soldier on the right is 17-year-old Thomas Wentworth from New Hampshire. The identity of the soldier below is unknown. To protect fragile ferrotypes, a type of image exposed directly onto a lacquered iron sheet, they were usually displayed in ornate, lidded frames. Chris Benedetto Collection.

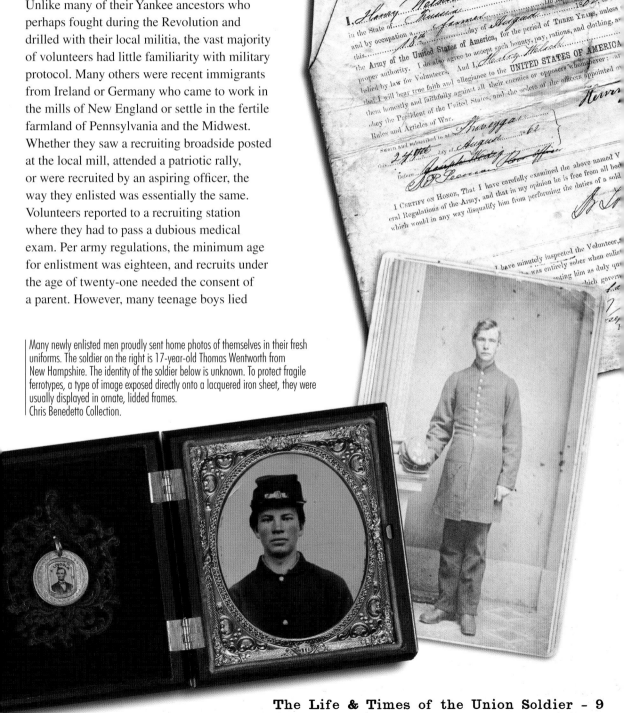

Volunteer! Volunteer!
AVOID THE DRAFT!

TO ARMS!   TO ARMS!

121st REGIMENT, P. V.

Accepted for Three Years or the War,

COL. CHAPMAN BIDDLE.

$160 BOUNTY
And 1 Month's Pay in Advance.

RECRUITS WANTED FOR COMP'Y D
AT THE
Anderson House, 1529 South St.

OPPOSITE KATER MARKET

J. G. ROSENGARTEN,
RECRUITING OFFICER.

about their age to circumvent this requirement. Likewise, according to regulations, men over forty-five could not enlist, yet the rosters of many regiments show dozens of soldiers above this age.

Once they had officially enlisted, the green recruits reported to a camp of rendezvous where they were molded into disciplined soldiers. The infantry regiment was the most important basic fighting unit of the Civil War, and the typical size of a regiment at the beginning of the conflict was approximately 1,000 men, divided into ten companies designated by letters (A, B, C, etc). Each company consisted largely of privates, one fifer, and one drummer. The chain of command in each company included eight corporals and five sergeants who received their orders from a few lieutenants and their captain. These officers ultimately reported to the major, adjutant, and the colonel, who issued general orders in writing, inspired his soldiers before a battle, and directed a bugler to played various

calls when verbal commands could not be heard over the chaos of combat or across long distances. Other commissioned officers in a typical regiment included a lieutenant-colonel, a regimental surgeon, and a quartermaster responsible for issuing equipment and rations. Many regiments also left their home states with brass bands to keep up the morale and entertain the troops, but most of them were soon discharged. Disease and combat took a heavy toll. By the end of 1862, the average size of a fighting regiment was no more than three to four hundred soldiers and officers.

When the war began, equipping, feeding, and supplying an army of this magnitude was a task far beyond the manufacturing capacity of the existing Union arsenals, and demanded the industrial might of the North. Civilian mills were quickly converted to produce millions of uniforms, shoes, accouterments, weapons, and ammunition. In the end, the Confederacy was overwhelmed not only by the relentless industrial war machine of the North and the enormous size of its armies, but also by Union soldiers who were determined to preserve the United States, and for some, eradicate slavery from American society.

Opposite: This recruitment broadside printed in Philadelphia, PA, clearly shows that money was an important factor in many men's decision to enlist. Below: A view of the Antietam National Battlefield in Sharpsburg, MD.

THE SOLDIER'S DRESS & EQUIPMENT

The Soldier's Dress & Equipment

By late 1861, state-issue uniforms and equipment worn by Union troops were, with few exceptions, replaced by mass-produced clothing and gear distributed by four major Federal arsenals in New York, Philadelphia, Cincinnati, and St. Louis, creating the appearance of the average soldier notable for its overall uniformity with subtle modifications of army guidelines. Here is a typical Union infantryman as he may have appeared in 1862, standing at "attention" and viewed from the back at "right-shoulder shift," two of the most common positions in the 1860s Manual of Arms.

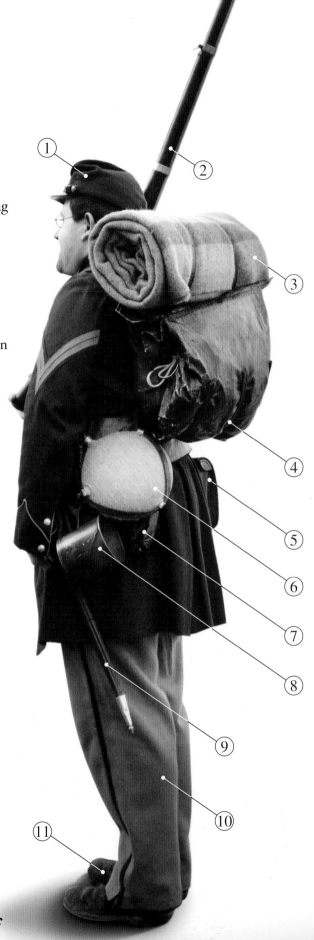

1. Forage Cap
2. Springfield Rifle Musket
3. Blanket
4. Knapsack
5. Cartridge Box
6. Canteen
7. Haversack
8. Tin Cup
9. Bayonet Scabbard
10. Trousers
11. Brogans
12. Corporal Stripes
13. Issue Coat
14. Belt Plate
15. Waist Belt
16. Bayonet
17. Cap Pouch

1

3

2

12

13

14

15

16

17

Issue Coats

The two wool coats pictured here were the most widely worn. Above is the four-button, lined fatigue blouse or "sack" coat issued to soldiers in four regulation sizes, often requiring alterations. Some tore out the brown lining that was too warm during the summer and used it as a gun rag. On the facing page is the nine-button army dress coat, patterned after the popular civilian fashion of the mid-nineteenth century. Photographs of dead soldiers at the battle of Gettysburg in July 1863 tragically demonstrate that, despite their formal appearance, these handsome coats were worn in the field throughout the year. The wool chevrons hand-sewn onto the sleeves indicate the rank of corporal.

18 - Union Soldier of the Civil War

Great Coat

The impressive army-issue sky blue wool kersey great coat was issued to soldiers to protect them in winter weather. Thousands of soldiers wore this style of coat during the bloody battles at Fredericksburg, Virginia, and Stone's River, Tennessee, in December 1862.

Shirt

The army-issue shirt made from domet wool flannel was rough against the skin and sweltering in the summer, and thus not very popular among soldiers. Photographs and letters reveal that some soldiers had more comfortable civilian shirts sent from home as soon as they had the chance.

Trousers and Drawers

The U.S. Army Regulations of 1861 specified that trousers for enlisted infantrymen were to be made of dark blue wool. By mid-1862 however, supplies of indigo dye were running low, so the vast majority of trousers issued to volunteers were sky blue instead. Like other parts of the infantry uniform, trousers were often altered or hemmed by soldiers in the field for a better fit. Suspenders or braces, like the "poor boy" style shown here, were added if the waist was too loose. Trousers worn by non-commissioned officers had a dark blue stripe down the outer seam, half an inch wide for corporals and an inch wide for sergeants. White cotton flannel drawers were issued in three sizes; they helped soldiers keep out the cold and prevented chafing from their wool trousers during the summer. But, as with shirts and socks, some soldiers preferred to wear civilian drawers sent from home, or none at all.

Socks and Brogans

Army-issue leather shoes were probably the most despised accouterment due to their poor fit and shoddy quality. They were mass-produced and had thin soles that were either hand sewn, machine sewn, or pegged with wooden nails. Although the Army Regulations of 1861 specified that soldiers should be issued four pairs per year, many wore holes through the leather, or even went barefoot before receiving a new pair. Soldiers did not always receive their allowance of wool socks in a timely manner either. They often requested more comfortable hand-knit socks from home. National organizations, such as the U.S. Sanitary Commission, and local aid societies, sent thousands of pairs to camps and hospitals.

U.S. Model 1861
Springfield Rifle Musket

This was the most common and perhaps the most popular firearm issued to Union infantrymen, primarily because it was reliable in the field, and noticeably lighter than similar muzzle-loading muskets imported from Europe. Made of burnished steel, with an American black walnut stock, the .58 caliber Model 1861 weighed about 9 pounds without the bayonet. It was fitted with a sight for use at 300 and 500 yards, an indication of its deadly range. By 1863, even though the Federal Armory in Springfield, Massachusetts, was producing 250,000 rifles annually, to keep up with the enormous demand, the government had to contract with several arms makers in cities including Manchester, New Hampshire, Providence, Rhode Island, and Hartford, Connecticut. Altogether, over 1.5 million Springfield-model firearms were produced. At the end of the war, volunteers leaving the service were allowed to purchase their rifles from the government for six dollars each. Today, original Springfield rifle muskets in good condition are worth thousands of dollars.

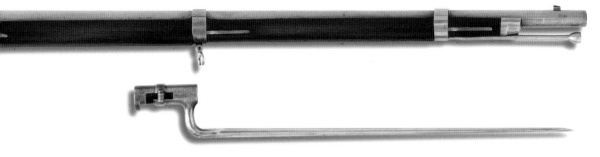

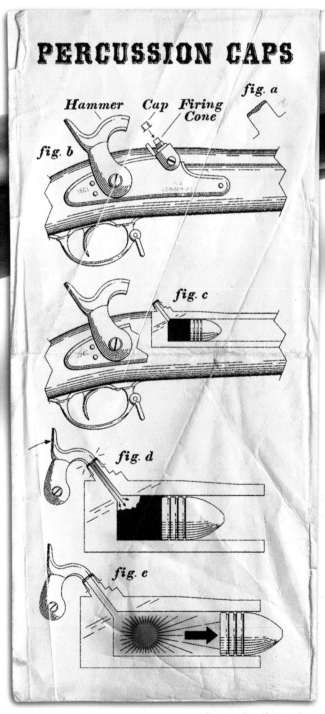

PERCUSSION CAPS

Hammer **Cap** **Firing Cone**

fig. a

fig. b

fig. c

fig. d

fig. e

Fig. a: The percussion cap is a brass or copper cap containing a small amount of mercury fulminate, an explosive compound highly sensitive to shocks.

Fig. b: The hammer is cocked and the percussion cap is fitted over the firing cone.

Fig. c: The firing cone leads to the breech, where the gunpowder charge is loaded.

Fig. d: When the percussion cap is struck by the hammer, the mercury fulminate detonates.

Fig. e: The detonation, communicated through the firing cone, sets off the charge.

THE MINIE BALL

The Civil War introduced America to a devastating new type of bullet that combined increased range with the loading speed of the smoothbore musket and the accuracy of the rifle. The Minié ball was named after its French inventor Claude-Étienne Minié. Its main feature was a hollow base designed to expand in the barrel upon firing.

a) The undersized bullet is easily rammed down the barrel in spite of the rifling or residue.

b) The deflagration of the gunpowder flares out the skirt at the base of the bullet.

c) This produces a very tight fit against the rifling of the barrel, resulting in increased velocity and accuracy.

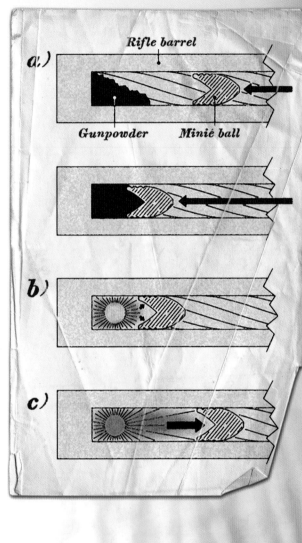

a.)

Rifle barrel

Gunpowder   Minié ball

b)

c)

Paper Cartridges

Thousands of women, eager to contribute to the war effort, worked in "laboratories" preparing millions of paper cartridges. The grooves of the lead bullets were filled with a lubricating mixture of tallow and beeswax. Each bullet was then wrapped in paper along with a carefully measured amount of gunpowder to form a cartridge. The cartridges were packaged in bundles of ten that included a paper tube with twelve percussion caps. The extra caps could be used in case of misfire, or without a charge to clear the firing cone.

Cartridge Box

The cartridge box was slung across the chest and
rested on the right hip within easy grasp during
battle. Inside the leather box were two tins that
held loose cartridges on top and bundles of ten in
the lower compartments. These metal containers
and two leather flaps effectively protected the paper
cartridges from moisture in inclement weather. For much of
the war, the outer flap was punched with two holes to secure
the "US" box plate made of lead stamped with polished brass.
Another feature common to all patterns of boxes was a sewn
implement pocket where soldiers stored cloth patches and
various tools used to maintain and clean the rifle after firing.

RIFLE, MUSKET & RIFLE, 58
65 GRAINS M POWDER

Waist Belt

Black leather belts were issued to Union troops for utilitarian reasons, because they carried two important accouterments: the cap pouch and bayonet scabbard. Early in the war, belts were issued with a leather "keeper" that forced the wearer either to step into the loosened belt or put it on over his head. Finding this an inconvenience, many soldiers simply cut the keeper off. Beginning in mid-1863, the army followed this trend by fitting new detachable brass keepers that made the belt much more practical.

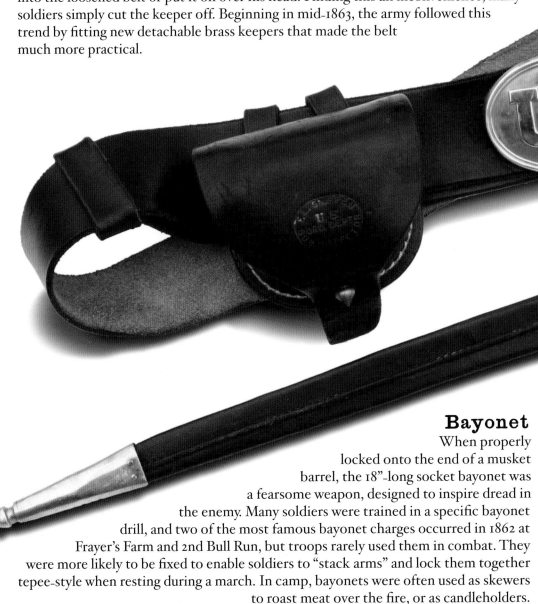

Bayonet

When properly locked onto the end of a musket barrel, the 18"-long socket bayonet was a fearsome weapon, designed to inspire dread in the enemy. Many soldiers were trained in a specific bayonet drill, and two of the most famous bayonet charges occurred in 1862 at Frayer's Farm and 2nd Bull Run, but troops rarely used them in combat. They were more likely to be fixed to enable soldiers to "stack arms" and lock them together tepee-style when resting during a march. In camp, bayonets were often used as skewers to roast meat over the fire, or as candleholders.

Belt Plate

Like the one on the cartridge box, the infantry waist belt plate was made of lead stamped with brass that each soldier was expected to keep polished. A tarnished belt or box plate was possibly an indicator of poor morale or discipline within a regiment. Although the heavy belt plate was mostly ornamental, some surviving examples clearly show signs that they have stopped Confederate bullets, thereby saving the lives of the soldiers wearing them.

Rifle Maintenance

Soldiers were expected to maintain their firearms because they were government property, but having a clean, functioning weapon was also a matter of pride and could mean the difference between life or death on the battlefield. The wiper (1) was screwed onto the end of the ramrod. A strip of cloth (2) was passed through it and pushed down the barrel to clean out gunpowder residue. After heavy fighting, soldiers sometimes poured hot water boiled on the campfire down the bore, dumped it out, and then wiped the bore dry with as many cloth patches as necessary. If a bullet was lodged in the barrel, the ball-screw or puller (3) was employed to remove the obstruction. The musket tool (4) was used as a screwdriver to disassemble the weapon for maintenance. It featured a wrench to unscrew the firing cone, which was cleaned out with a cone pick (5). When the barrel of the musket was clean and lightly oiled to prevent rust, a wood and brass tampion (6) was placed in the muzzle to keep moisture out.

Cap Pouch

Various designs were developed during the war, but the cap pouches' basic purpose remained unchanged: to store items which all percussion muskets required in order to fire — the caps. Constructed of leather, each pouch had an outer flap that closed with a brass button riveted to the bottom. Inside was a lining of sheepskin with wool to prevent the caps from falling out, as well as a small leather loop or slot for the cone pick (5) where a soldier could easily find it during battle.

1. A paper cartridge is retrieved from the cartridge box.

2. The cartridge is torn with the teeth. A few opposable front teeth were among the few physical requirements to enlist.

3. The gunpowder is poured into the barrel, and the bullet is inserted.

4. Soldiers were trained to ram the charge with a single finger to limit injuries in case of an accidental discharge.

5. The hammer is pulled to half-cock, a safety position that reveals the firing cone.

6. A percussion cap is retrieved from the cap pouch.

7. The percussion cap is fitted to the firing cone.

8. The hammer is fully cocked, and the musket is ready to be fired.

Firing the Musket

Manuals of arms defined as many as nine distinct commands to load, aim, and discharge muskets. Although these were the object of relentless drill on parade grounds, the chaotic reality of the battlefields usually demanded a less ceremonious approach. It was never very long before soldiers began to fire at will either under order, or by necessity.

Forage cap

The Model 1858 forage cap was by far the most common kind of headgear. Constructed of lightweight dark blue wool, it often proved too thin in the winter and too hot in the summer. Soldiers were constantly devising ways to cool off, including wearing damp handkerchiefs under their caps, or punching air holes into the circular cardboard crowns. Some caps were even fitted with a circular metal ventilator. The stiff leather visor offered little protection from the sun or bad weather, and wartime images reveal that the adjustable chin strap was rarely used. In the field, many soldiers proudly wore brass numbers and letters on their caps to indicate their regiment and company.

In 1863, army corps received their own insignias, which became immensely popular and were worn on caps until the end of the war.

Camp Hat

Civilian "smoking" or "lounging" hats like this plush green velvet example were very popular with soldiers when they were off duty and could relax in camp, lighting up a pipe, reading a newspaper, or perhaps playing cards. Of course, these were not army-issued, they were handmade by the soldier's wife, sister, or mother and usually embroidered with great skill.

Knapsack

Constructed of painted linen or cotton, bridle leather straps, and brass hardware, the Model 1855 "double bag" knapsack above was issued to Union troops to carry their extra gear. Either the issue wool blanket or the great coat, was strapped to the top of the pack, and two compartments or bags inside typically contained an extra shirt, pair of socks, drawers, shelter half, rubber blanket, and personal belongings. As rookie soldiers became hardened veterans, they soon learned to lighten their load before a long march, or even discard their heavy knapsack altogether.

Shelter Half

Each soldier typically carried a
canvas "half" initially issued in early
1862 with bone or tin buttons.
Two shelter halves were buttoned together
and pitched with wooden poles and stakes
to make a full tent barely large
enough for two men.

Gum Blanket

This practical piece of gear was highly valued by Union soldiers because it functioned
effectively as a ground cloth or tent in the field. In the rain, it could also be worn by
running a leather shoelace or metal hook through the brass grommets, and throwing
it over the head. Gum blankets were made of cotton that either had one side coated in
the same black varnish as the knapsack or were rubberized by a process patented by
Charles Goodyear in 1844.

TENT CITIES

In this rarely published photo, Union troops in Petersburg, Virginia, mingle in their camp on a sunny day toward the end of winter or early spring during the last year of the war. The season can be inferred from the trees, and from the stick and mud chimneys venting fires that heated the tents. During the cooler months of the year, many regiments also built makeshift ovens to bake loaves of soft bread, a welcome relief from almost inedible hardtack. The slouching soldier in the foreground, who seems to be taking a nap, used at least one rubber blanket to keep cold blasts of air out of his tent. The distinctive insignia sewn on his sleeve and the shovel lying next to him indicates that this soldier, and probably the others nearby, were pioneers who helped design and build enormous defensive earthworks and wooden structures like those seen in the back. On the right side of the image, soldiers take advantage of the sunshine to dry their damp blankets on top of their tents.

Haversack

This vital piece of equipment carried the soldier's rations, eating utensils, and other personal items. Like the government-issue knapsack, most haversacks were made of heavy linen or cotton waterproofed with glossy black varnish that often got sticky in the summer heat and contaminated the food inside. Buttoned to the inside was a cloth bag or pocket that could be removed and washed at the soldier's discretion.

Canteen

Keeping their tin-plated canteen filled with three pints of clean drinking water was a constant battle for Union soldiers. Tainted water caused deadly diseases, including dysentery and typhoid. While there were some minor variations, most canteens were covered with wool cloth to keep the water cool in summer. Canteens were fitted with a leather strap until 1863, when white cotton straps became more common. Many soldiers shortened or tied knots in their straps so their canteens would not swing wildly during rapid maneuvers.

Mittens

Trigger-finger mittens were essential during the long, cold winters as soldiers grasped their icy weapons. Many troops received them from home based on instructions printed in newspapers from Ohio to Maine. Private manufacturers also contracted with the army to knit thousands of mittens, including entrepreneur Abby Condon of Penobscot, Maine, who paid 25¢ per pair to eager volunteers across New England.

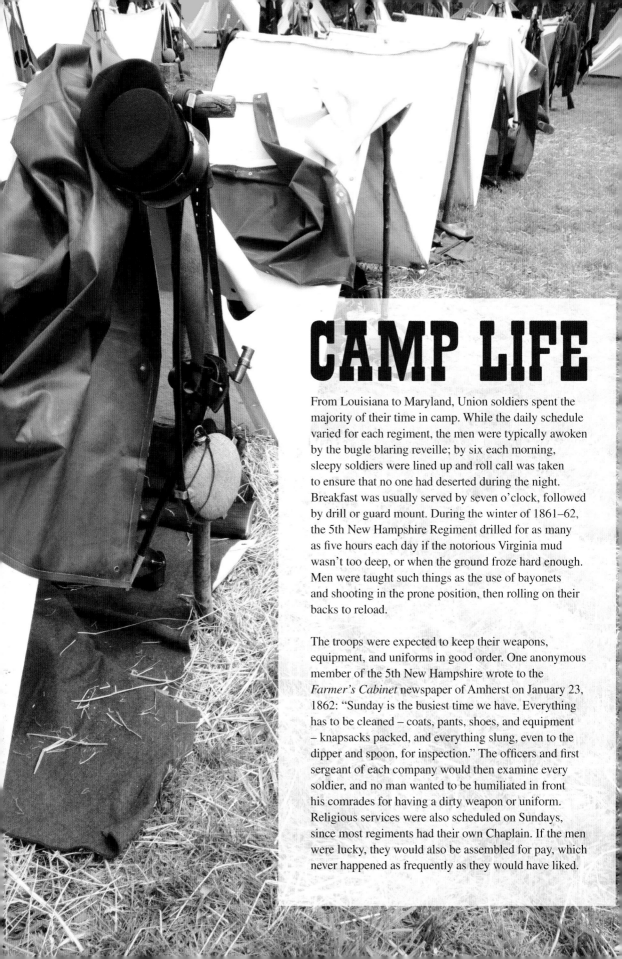

CAMP LIFE

From Louisiana to Maryland, Union soldiers spent the majority of their time in camp. While the daily schedule varied for each regiment, the men were typically awoken by the bugle blaring reveille; by six each morning, sleepy soldiers were lined up and roll call was taken to ensure that no one had deserted during the night. Breakfast was usually served by seven o'clock, followed by drill or guard mount. During the winter of 1861–62, the 5th New Hampshire Regiment drilled for as many as five hours each day if the notorious Virginia mud wasn't too deep, or when the ground froze hard enough. Men were taught such things as the use of bayonets and shooting in the prone position, then rolling on their backs to reload.

The troops were expected to keep their weapons, equipment, and uniforms in good order. One anonymous member of the 5th New Hampshire wrote to the *Farmer's Cabinet* newspaper of Amherst on January 23, 1862: "Sunday is the busiest time we have. Everything has to be cleaned – coats, pants, shoes, and equipment – knapsacks packed, and everything slung, even to the dipper and spoon, for inspection." The officers and first sergeant of each company would then examine every soldier, and no man wanted to be humiliated in front his comrades for having a dirty weapon or uniform. Religious services were also scheduled on Sundays, since most regiments had their own Chaplain. If the men were lucky, they would also be assembled for pay, which never happened as frequently as they would have liked.

On holidays such as Christmas, Thanksgiving, or St. Patrick's Day, games and special dinners were enjoyed by many regiments to break up the monotony and raise morale. On January 2, 1862, an unidentified soldier in the 5th New Hampshire wrote home to the *Farmer's Cabinet* that on Christmas Day there was "nothing but fun in the Fifth. The programme was the one laid for Thanksgiving. In the forenoon, a foot race and wrestling match for prizes. An oyster dinner and afterward, a sack race and scramble for a greased pig. One of our boys caught the pig and bore him off in triumph." Describing the celebration of the Irish holiday in the Army of the Potomac on March 20, 1863, the *Daily National Intelligencer* in Washington reported that the day began with religious services in honor of St. Patrick, followed by horse races on a mile-long course; in the afternoon, there was also supposed to be "a foot race, a sack race, a wheelbarrow match, and a pig chase ... but at four o'clock the festivities were brought to a close."

On a typical late afternoon, an entire regiment was assembled for the ceremonial dress parade, during which the colonel shared news or orders with his men. Then came supper, and all lights were out by nine at night. During the intervening hours, officers studied the drill manuals and tested their knowledge, while enlisted men found ways of making their camps as comfortable as possible. Before they were issued shelter halves, troops were often quartered in Sibley tents complete with wooden floors and iron woodstoves. Each of these large, teepee-shaped tents could accommodate up to twenty men. Later in the war, timber cabins roofed with canvas were erected, not much different than the ones at Valley

Forge nearly a century earlier. But generally, Union soldiers fared much better in the winters than their Revolutionary predecessors. The same 5th New Hampshire soldier mentioned earlier vividly commented in January 1862: "I wish you could take a peep at us tonight in our snug, cosy quarters ... about half are writing, some reading, and some building castles to live in when the war is over. We are a merry set of fellows having all the necessaries of life and some of its luxuries. Now sir, I have yet to see the first soldier who does not get everything he needs in the way of rations or clothing." By the end of the summer, after he had experienced the rigors of life on the march, it's likely this Yankee soldier had changed his opinion. Colonel Edward Cross observed in his official report after the battle of Antietam on October 31, 1862, that his surviving men "were weary, ragged, many of them barefooted and without overcoats or blankets, only the tattered remains of shelter tents."

Canteen Half

While tinned iron plates were issued by the army, some troops used bowl-shaped canteen halves, yet another example of their ingenuity. Canteens found on the battlefield were placed in the campfire. The heat melted the solder and separated the two metal halves into bowls. A stick or piece of wire was then attached as a handle, and the former canteen was used as a makeshift fry pan or basin. The canteen half easily slid inside haversacks or knapsacks.

Fry Pan

While troops on campaign often discarded any non-essential gear to lighten their load, they were very reluctant to part with their sheet iron fry pan or skillet. Books and letters from the war reveal that groups of soldiers in the same company typically formed a "mess" and purchased a fry pan from a sutler or local blacksmith. On the march, the men took turns carrying the fry pan strapped to their knapsacks, where it was out of the way but within easy reach when they started a fire to prepare a tasty meal after a long, tiring day.

Cutlery

The soldier's cutlery was issued by the army, purchased, or obtained through aid societies. On January 16, 1862, the *Ripley Bee* of Ripley, Ohio, asked those "benevolent persons who are knitting socks for the soldiers" to also send "half a dozen postage stamps, a plug of tobacco, a short pipe, a pair of woolen mittens, a knife, fork, and spoon ... and any other little things useful for a bachelor." Also common were various knife, fork, and spoon sets, which sold for about a dollar. The popular folding design shown here was made by the Union Knife Company of Naugatuck, Connecticut.

Tin Cup

Described during the war as a "boiler" or "dipper," this versatile piece of equipment was often strapped to the haversack so a soldier could easily grab it to brew his coffee or tea; boil a stew with beef, potatoes, and crushed hardtack; or, if they were in camp, cook baked beans flavored with salt pork. Made of tin-plated sheet iron, these cups quickly turned black over the fire.

Hardtack

This legendary cracker, consisting of flour, water, and salt, was the main staple of the soldier's diet because, if kept dry, it could be preserved almost indefinitely. Before a campaign, troops were typically issued three days' worth of rations, including thirty pieces of hardtack that they somehow crammed into their haversacks. It was eaten in a variety of ways; "raw" with some sugar on top, crumbled into a cup to thicken a stew, or even softened with water and fried in grease rendered from salt pork. Hardtack was distributed in large wooden crates weighing up to 50 pounds. Empty crates were, tragically, often used as makeshift coffins and grave markers for men who had once joked that hardtack was tough enough to stop bullets.

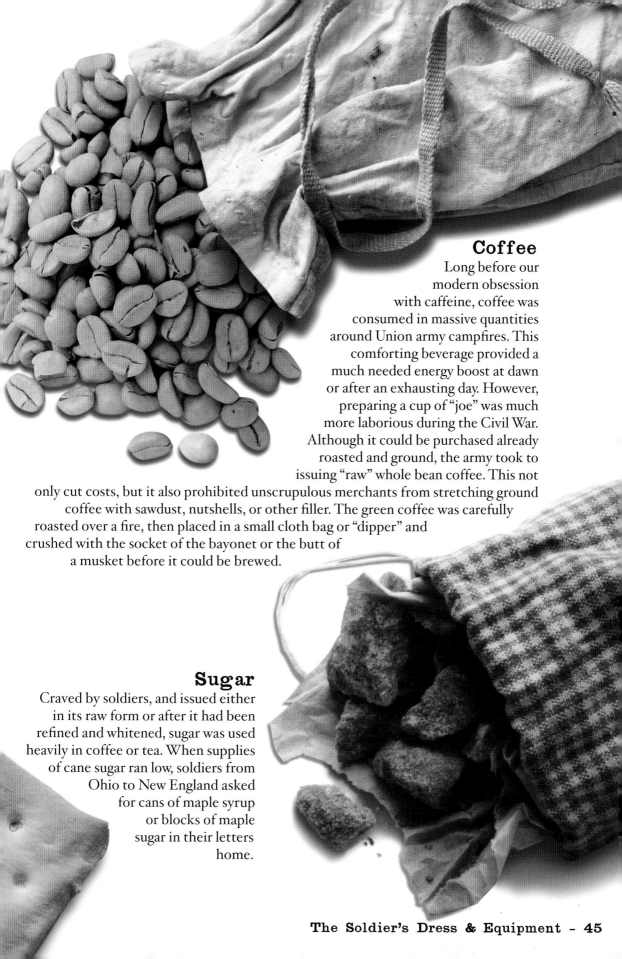

Coffee

Long before our modern obsession with caffeine, coffee was consumed in massive quantities around Union army campfires. This comforting beverage provided a much needed energy boost at dawn or after an exhausting day. However, preparing a cup of "joe" was much more laborious during the Civil War. Although it could be purchased already roasted and ground, the army took to issuing "raw" whole bean coffee. This not only cut costs, but it also prohibited unscrupulous merchants from stretching ground coffee with sawdust, nutshells, or other filler. The green coffee was carefully roasted over a fire, then placed in a small cloth bag or "dipper" and crushed with the socket of the bayonet or the butt of a musket before it could be brewed.

Sugar

Craved by soldiers, and issued either in its raw form or after it had been refined and whitened, sugar was used heavily in coffee or tea. When supplies of cane sugar ran low, soldiers from Ohio to New England asked for cans of maple syrup or blocks of maple sugar in their letters home.

Salt Pork

"Sowbelly" was perhaps the most common meat issued to Northern soldiers, though they also frequently ate fresh beef or chickens foraged from local farms. To prevent spoilage, salt pork barrels were filled with brine or lard. Soldiers often boiled the meat to temper the overpowering salty flavor. On the march, pork was roasted quickly over a fire at the end of a bayonet or fried in a plate or canteen half. Occasionally, soldiers engaged in "pig hunts" as they marched through the Southern countryside; in late 1862, William McCarter of 116th Pennsylvania Infantry captured a 40-pound piglet, dispatched it with his bayonet, and carried it away in his gum blanket.

Rice and Potatoes

These starches offered a variety of culinary options to Union soldiers. Rice was typically thrown into a stew, or cooked by itself with some sugar, as described by Massachusetts officer Charles Brewster in May 1862. Potatoes could be diced and fried with grease from salt pork, boiled, or baked over a campfire. Though potatoes were often issued, it was not uncommon for troops to pick potato fields clean as they marched across the Confederacy. One member of the 38th Indiana Regiment compared his fellow soldiers to an "army of locusts, for nothing eatable escaped us."

Dried Beans and Peas

Beans were among the most popular foods, and were often prepared in quantities large enough to feed an entire company or even regiment. On August 3, 1861, the *Bangor Daily Whig* of Maine described how soldiers from that state dug a hole that they filled each evening with hot embers and a large pot filled with beans, water, and salt pork. In the morning, the beans were "cooked in an excellent manner." Another soldier, drummer boy William Bircher of Minnesota, wrote in his diary of how his regiment enjoyed baked beans, hardtack, coffee, and sowbelly for their Christmas dinner, 1862. On occasion, soldiers were also issued dried peas, which they prepared in a similar manner. In many Union camps, the bugle call for breakfast was nicknamed "Peas on a Trencher."

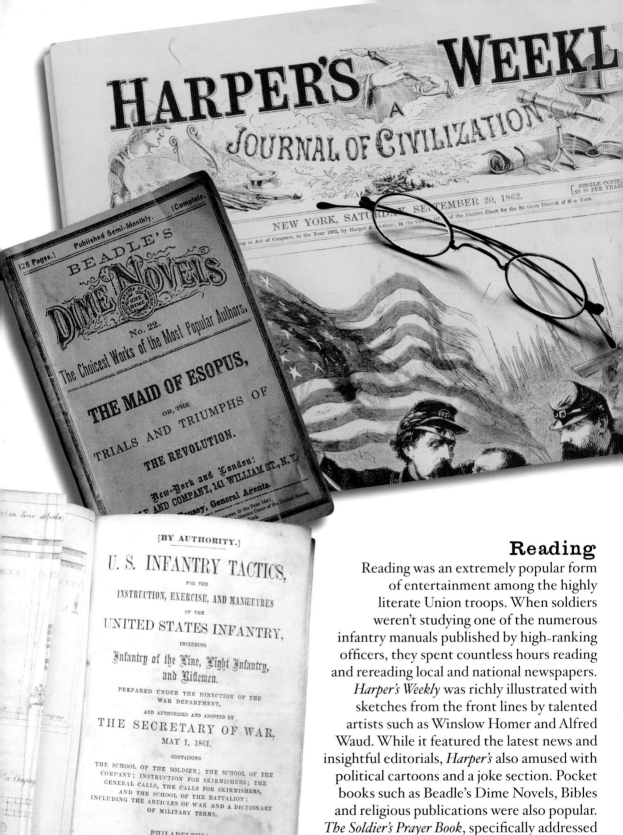

Reading

Reading was an extremely popular form of entertainment among the highly literate Union troops. When soldiers weren't studying one of the numerous infantry manuals published by high-ranking officers, they spent countless hours reading and rereading local and national newspapers. *Harper's Weekly* was richly illustrated with sketches from the front lines by talented artists such as Winslow Homer and Alfred Waud. While it featured the latest news and insightful editorials, *Harper's* also amused with political cartoons and a joke section. Pocket books such as Beadle's Dime Novels, Bibles and religious publications were also popular. *The Soldier's Prayer Book*, specifically addressed the spiritual welfare of those who faced the terrifying prospect of combat and death on the battlefield.

BATTLE FLAGS

1861 regulations permitted each infantry regiment to carry a national flag, plus another identifying the regiment. These flags were made of silk or cotton, each nearly 6 feet square. Early in the war, many flags were carefully crafted by groups of patriotic women and presented at grand ceremonies. The state banner of the 20th New York Regiment, for instance, reminded all those who gazed upon it that it had been "presented by the ladies of Poughkeepsie."

While the "colors" were intended to help identify regiments in the chaos of the battlefield, they also embodied the soldiers' pride in their state and their cause. Each regiment had a "color guard" made of two "color bearers" with the rank of sergeant, and eight armed corporals whose sole duty in battle was to protect the flags. The soldiers selected for this prestigious duty were usually the most distinguished and courageous in their regiment. In battle, each side often targeted the other's color guard, hoping to break the morale of the enemy or even capture their flags. It was considered a great dishonor to allow one's colors to fall into enemy hands, and soldiers went to great lengths to prevent it. In July 1863 at Gettysburg, the color guard of the 16th Maine Infantry tore their silk colors into small pieces and stuffed them into their pockets before they were overwhelmed by Confederate forces. Likewise, capturing the flag of an enemy unit was a glorious feat of arms. After color corporal George Nettleton of the 5th New Hampshire Volunteers captured the state flag of the 4th North Carolina at the battle of Antietam, he was quickly promoted to the rank of lieutenant. In a strange twist of fate, Nettleton was killed while raising the state colors of his own regiment four months later, in December 1862. That same year, the government authorized regiments to add lists of battles to their national flags. In January 1863, Colonel Edward Cross of the 5th New Hampshire commissioned a new national flag, inscribed with nine battles, from Fair Oaks to Fredericksburg.

Many captured banners were returned to their respective states at the end of the war. But in some case, they were held as spoils of war for many decades. The flag captured by George Nettleton at Antietam wasn't returned by New Hampshire to North Carolina until 1914, and Georgia did not return the 17th Maine Regiment's colors until 1998.

Still noticeable today on many surviving Civil War flags is the blood of the soldiers who carried them, a poignant reminder of the brave men who were severely wounded or sacrificed their lives on Civil War battlefields.

A gallant color-bearer. The September 1862 cover of *Harper's Weekly* pays homage to H. Alexander, the color bearer of the 10th New York Regiment whose devotion was so strong that the colors could not be pried from his tenacious grasp, even as he was taken unconscious after receiving three terrible wounds.

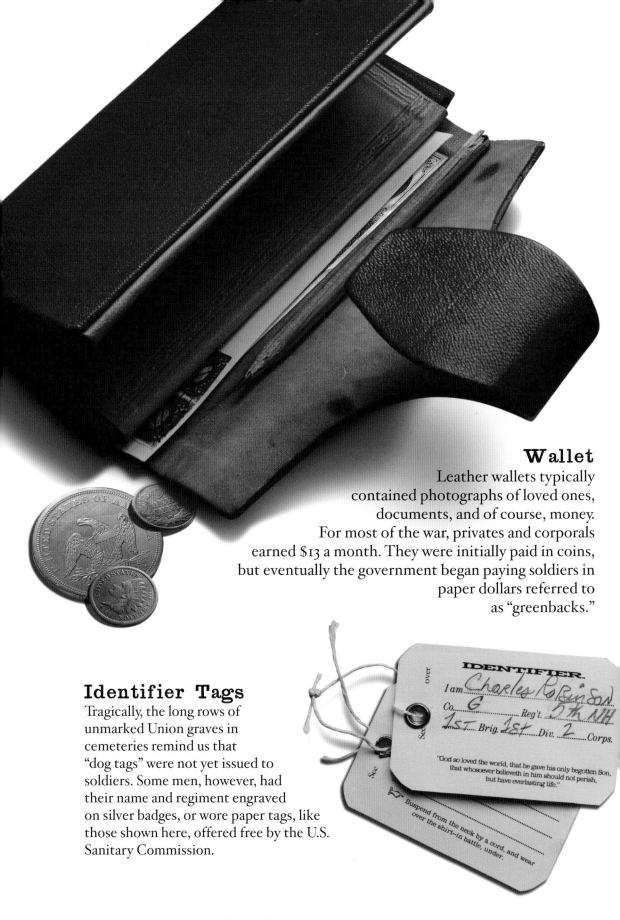

Wallet

Leather wallets typically contained photographs of loved ones, documents, and of course, money. For most of the war, privates and corporals earned $13 a month. They were initially paid in coins, but eventually the government began paying soldiers in paper dollars referred to as "greenbacks."

Identifier Tags

Tragically, the long rows of unmarked Union graves in cemeteries remind us that "dog tags" were not yet issued to soldiers. Some men, however, had their name and regiment engraved on silver badges, or wore paper tags, like those shown here, offered free by the U.S. Sanitary Commission.

IDENTIFIER.
I am Charles Robinson
Co. G   Reg't. 5th NH
1st Brig. 1st Div. 2 Corps.

"God so loved the world, that he gave his only begotten Son, that whosoever believeth in him should not perish, but have everlasting life."

Suspend from the neck by a cord, and wear over the shirt-in battle, under.

Union Jack sending one of Jeff Davis' Pirates to "Davy Jones locker"—Serves 'em right.

D. Murphy's Son, Print. 88 Fulton-st. N. Y.

Pvt. George Putnam
5th NH Vols.
Richardson's Div.
Army of the Potomac
Washington D.C.

Mail

"Mail call" was highly anticipated by Union soldiers, who often received letters, hand-knitted socks, and even pies from home during the holidays. Family and friends eagerly awaited news that their beloved soldier had survived the latest battle, or had recovered from illness but, sadly, many letters were written by fellow soldiers or officers reporting that a father, son, or husband had died.

Photographs

While photography dawned in America around 1840, its popularity exploded in 1861, when millions of soldiers and civilians had their "likenesses" taken. This image, likely the young wife or sister of a Union volunteer, is a carte de visite (CDV), which was the most common type of photograph produced during the war.

Wet Collodion Photography

The wet collodion process pioneered by Englishman Frederick Scott Archer during the 1850s marked a significant step forward in the emerging science of photography.

The process became faster, and produced finely detailed images. For the first time, photographic portraits became affordable to almost everyone, and studios spread to every corner of the country. Collodion is a syrupy solution of nitrocellulose that served as a substrate for the photosensitive chemicals. From the moment the collodion plate was prepared, the photographer had ten minutes at most to expose and develop the plate,

before the collodion would dry out and lose its sensitivity. For lack of practical metering devices, photographers relied entirely on experience and guesswork to determine exposure times that ranged from a few second to several minutes. The limitations of the technology imposed a number of restrictions and hardships on the Civil War field photographer. Since the plates had to be prepared in almost complete darkness and within minutes of exposure, photographers did much of their work in small, horse-drawn darkrooms or black tents. In hot weather, the stifling air inside, laced with volatile chemicals, made for dreadful working conditions.

Collodion photography affords a vivid look into the 19th century, yet it can also contribute to a somewhat tainted perception of the period. Exposure times of several seconds precluded any sort of candid, or action shot. Photos were carefully staged, often resulting in stiff attitudes, and stern faces. Furthermore, the process interprets colors in peculiar ways: Light blues are indistinguishable from white, while reds and yellows darken almost to black. As a result, skies always seem cloudless, and a lady in a festive dress of reds and yellows might appear to be wearing black as if in mourning.

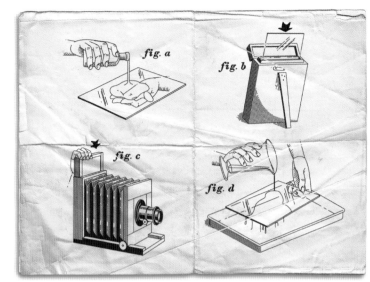

Fig. a: The collodion mixture is poured onto a glass plate to form an even coat. It is allowed to set for a few minutes. Fig. b: In a darkroom, the collodion plate is sensitized in a bath of silver salts. Fig. c: The plate is transported to the camera in a light-proof case and exposed. Fig. d: Back in the darkroom, the plate is developed, fixed, and washed. The process forms layers of silver in light areas of the image. The bright silver can be viewed as a positive over a dark background or, owing to its opacity, it can be used as a negative to produce an almost unlimited number of prints.

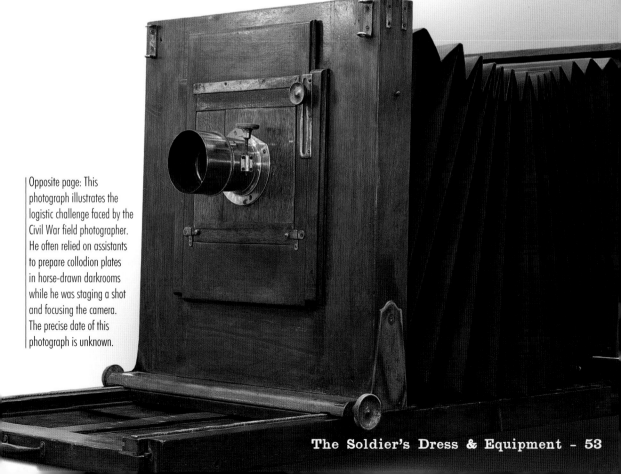

Opposite page: This photograph illustrates the logistic challenge faced by the Civil War field photographer. He often relied on assistants to prepare collodion plates in horse-drawn darkrooms while he was staging a shot and focusing the camera. The precise date of this photograph is unknown.

Toiletries Ditty Bag

The U.S. Army Regulations of 1861 stated that, where convenient, soldiers should bathe once or twice a week, but in the field, soldiers were a grimy group, splattered with blood, dirt, and gunpowder. When given the opportunity, they boiled their uniforms and bathed in rivers near camps. Many men carried small "ditty" bags in their knapsack containing soap, combs, toothbrushes, and shaving kits.

Bone Toothbrush

Toothbrushes had to be purchased from sutlers or sent from home. The poor nutrition many soldiers suffered often led to tooth loss. There are few photographs of Union soldiers showing their teeth, an indication that the men were well aware of the poor state of their dental hygiene.

Shaving Kit

By the 1860s, facial hair was fashionable, and this trend was reflected in the U.S. Army Regulations of 1861 that permitted soldiers to be clean shaven or keep their beards "neatly trimmed." On the march, they rarely had the opportunity to shave. They usually did so only after entering a well established camp or garrison.

Comb

Like razors and toothbrushes, combs were not issued by the army and had to be obtained independently. While army regulations dictated that hair was to be kept short to prevent the spread of lice, in reality few soldiers were not infested at some point in the course of their enlistment.

Button Cleaning Board

Soldiers used this handy tool to keep the tarnish off their coats when polishing their brass eagle buttons before an inspection. Sutlers sold a variety of commercial abrasives and polishes, but a rag or damp piece of leather dipped in wood ash from the campfire worked quite well in the field.

Playing Cards

Soldiers spent much more time in camp than in combat, and though it carried a negative social stigma, gambling remained a popular pastime throughout the war. The U.S. Army Regulations of 1861 stipulated that any officer who disbursed pay and who was discovered to "bet at cards or any game of hazard" had to be suspended from duty and turn over all the public funds in his possession.

Housewife

Often homemade by a soldier's wife, sister, or mother and presented as a parting gift, the "housewife," as it was commonly known during the war, was a small sewing kit that typically contained needles, thread, a folding pair of scissors, extra buttons, and cloth patches. The heavy wear and tear on uniforms during long marches and battles made these sewing kits indispensable for most soldiers.

CARING FOR THE SICK AND THE WOUNDED

When the war began, the Medical Department of the U.S. Army was wholly unprepared for the onslaught of wounded and sick soldiers that inundated military hospitals. Over the next four years, the government and independent volunteer organizations, such as the U.S. Sanitary Commission, worked continuously to improve the quality of care, a difficult task as battles grew larger and disease spread rampant through the ranks.

As early as May 1861, the Army's medical staff was deemed inadequate, and the governors of loyal states were authorized to appoint a surgeon and assistant surgeon for each volunteer regiment. By the summer of 1862, five thousand of them were serving in the Union Army, but like the soldiers for whom they cared, the vast majority had little or no experience in the military realm. Most were initially shocked by the horror and magnitude of their task.

One of the most daunting challenges was transporting wounded men off the battlefield. Early in the war this task was often left to other soldiers in the ranks or field musicians who were detailed as stretcher-bearers. Unfortunately, this haphazard system resulted in thousands of wounded soldiers being left on the battlefield for many hours or even days.

At the disastrous Union defeat at Bull Run in July 1861, John L. Rice of the 2nd New Hampshire Infantry was shot through the lung. He passed out from blood loss as his comrades tried to carry him off the field. Thinking him dead, and fearing capture, they left his body under a fence and ran. His regiment sent the tragic news to his family in New England, who held a funeral service in his honor. Two days later, Rice miraculously regained consciousness and discovered, to his horror, that maggots had infested his bloody wound. That evening, after spending the day caring for Southern casualties at a local church, a couple who lived nearby found Rice. For ten days, they cared for him, cleaning his wound and feeding him until he was well enough to be placed on a freight train to Richmond, where he became a prisoner of war until early 1862. Remarkably, he survived this ordeal and returned to the ranks to fight again.

In August 1862, to address the shameful problem of wounded soldiers being abandoned on the battlefield, Union officials created the Ambulance Corps. It was tasked with carrying casualties to the private homes, churches, or barns that were hurriedly converted into field hospitals. Each horse-drawn ambulance carried two stretchers, medical supplies, and a barrel of fresh water to quench the thirst of injured troops. For the wounded soldiers and the surgeons scrambling to save their lives, the sights, sounds, and smells were not soon forgotten. After Antietam in September 1862, Dr. Daniel Holt, assistant surgeon of the 121st New York Infantry, wrote to his wife: "Every

house, for miles around, is a hospital and I have seen arms, legs, feet, and hands lying in piles rotting in the blazing heat of a Southern sky unburied and uncared for, and still the knife went steadily in its work adding to the putrid mess."

In field hospitals across the South, thousands of men screamed in agony, and begged not to have their limbs amputated for fear of becoming invalids, unable to support their families. Most who refused amputation died from their wounds. For those who underwent the gruesome operations, a mixture of chloroform and ether was frequently used as an anesthetic. The mixture was poured onto a cloth placed over the mouth and nose. Some died from blood loss or even exposure to the anesthetic; others survived the amputation only to die from gangrene a few weeks later. Those fortunate enough to survive were eventually transported to larger hospitals in cities such as Washington, Philadelphia, New York, and Nashville where they were cared for by nurses who would even help them write letters to friends and relatives. Among the most famous of these volunteers were Clara Barton, who went on to organize the American Red Cross, and the poet Walt Whitman. Eventually, the army and individual states began helping thousands of discharged ex-soldiers transition back to civilian life. On October 10, 1862, for example, the *Daily Cleveland Herald* reported that volunteers planned to raise $100,000 "to procure artificial limbs for all Ohio volunteers maimed while in the service of their country."

Tragically, the majority of the nearly 360,000 deaths in the Union Army were not caused by battle wounds but by illnesses like malaria, dysentery, and typhoid that were contracted via mosquitoes or tainted drinking water. Physicians, unaware of how these diseases spread, failed to curb the deadly toll. To add to the problem, many Northerners found themselves in unfamiliar climates, facing germs to which they had no immunity. While some members of each regiment succumbed to sickness, one extreme example was the 16th New Hampshire Infantry, which suffered no combat casualties yet lost more than 200 men to disease in less than nine months in the bayous of Louisiana. John Rice, mentioned earlier, who had become a captain in this unit, described the awful scenes he witnessed: "Daily and hourly our boys sickened and died. Every morning they were found dead in their blankets … Time and again I saw them all accoutred for battle, with eyes to the front and musket in hand, stagger, sink to the ground where they had been standing, as dead as if shot in their tracks. Once, when a funeral squad had fired the last volley over the grave of a comrade, one of the squad moved forward, sank upon the fresh mound of his dead comrade and breathed his last. Another grave was hastily dug, another volley fired and that comrade was covered from sight."

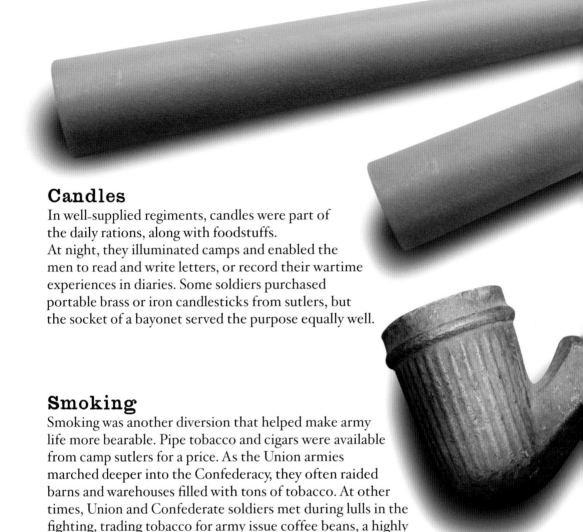

Candles

In well-supplied regiments, candles were part of
the daily rations, along with foodstuffs.
At night, they illuminated camps and enabled the
men to read and write letters, or record their wartime
experiences in diaries. Some soldiers purchased
portable brass or iron candlesticks from sutlers, but
the socket of a bayonet served the purpose equally well.

Smoking

Smoking was another diversion that helped make army
life more bearable. Pipe tobacco and cigars were available
from camp sutlers for a price. As the Union armies
marched deeper into the Confederacy, they often raided
barns and warehouses filled with tons of tobacco. At other
times, Union and Confederate soldiers met during lulls in the
fighting, trading tobacco for army issue coffee beans, a highly
prized commodity rarely available in the South. Clay pipes like
this one sold for as little as five cents each. Many soldiers took to
whittling pipes out of briarwood or laurel root. These pipes became a form of military
folk art that remains highly collectible today.

Tobacco Twist

Although it was already considered a nasty habit by some, chewing tobacco was
very popular with Union troops, partly because it could be carried easily in
a pocket and enjoyed in any kind of weather without matches or
fire. Produced in dozens of factories across Virginia and North
Carolina, a twist like the one shown here was typically
flavored with molasses, rum, cinnamon, or honey to
make it more palatable.

Matches

These essential articles, also known as "lucifers" during the war, had to be broken up and carried in a wooden or metallic match safe designed to protect its owner in case the very sensitive matches were ignited accidentally in a pocket. Matches often became scarce when Union armies were in the field, forcing soldiers to come up with ingenious ways to light their campfires, candles, and tobacco. While the 3rd New Hampshire Infantry was stationed in South Carolina, from 1861 to 1863, pieces of cotton were lit and passed from one smoker to the next to save matches.

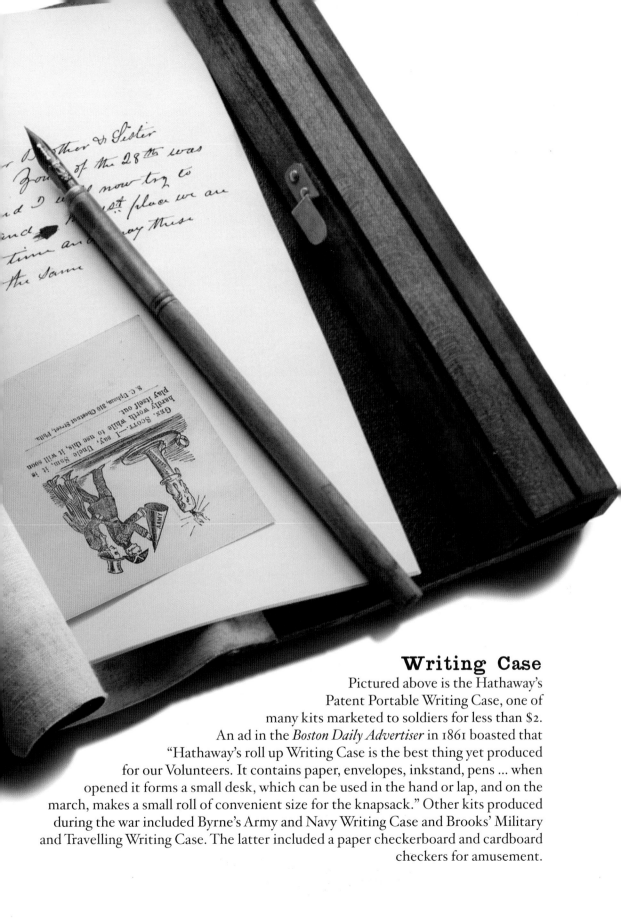

Writing Case

Pictured above is the Hathaway's
Patent Portable Writing Case, one of
many kits marketed to soldiers for less than $2.
An ad in the *Boston Daily Advertiser* in 1861 boasted that
"Hathaway's roll up Writing Case is the best thing yet produced
for our Volunteers. It contains paper, envelopes, inkstand, pens ... when
opened it forms a small desk, which can be used in the hand or lap, and on the
march, makes a small roll of convenient size for the knapsack." Other kits produced
during the war included Byrne's Army and Navy Writing Case and Brooks' Military
and Travelling Writing Case. The latter included a paper checkerboard and cardboard
checkers for amusement.

THE CONFEDERATE SOLDIER

"Reduced to the minimum, the private soldier consisted of one man, one hat, one jacket, one shirt, one pair of pants, one pair of drawers, one pair of shoes, and one pair of socks. His baggage was one blanket, one rubber blanket, and one haversack. The haversack generally contained smoking tobacco and a pipe, and a small piece of soap, with temporary additions of apples, persimmons, blackberries, and such other commodities as he could pick up on the march." With that, Carlton McCarthy, an artillery private in the Army of Northern Virginia, described what became the standard for soldiers in every branch of the Confederate army. Early in the war Southern troops were as well uniformed and equipped as their Northern counterparts, but as the war dragged on, soldiers and civilians had to cope with severe shortages of every kind.

Before the conflict, the agricultural Southern states depended heavily on the North for manufactured goods. The Confederate government was quick to send representatives to Europe to trade Southern cotton and tobacco for the latest in arms and military supplies. In response, the U.S. Navy blockaded every major Southern port. Furthermore, with the majority of the male population serving in the military, and with farmlands devastated by battles or deliberately set on fire, less food was grown each year, and less cotton, tobacco, or other crops were produced for export. Soldiers became used the hardships of campaign life; the shortages of food, clothing, and equipment, marching for hundreds of miles, sleeping out in the open in any weather. Being "reduced to the minimum" became a way of life. Much of what they needed, they readily took from the backs of the enemy, often preferring the better made Northern equipment to their own. Battlefields were littered with war materiel, and the soldiers frequently preferred to "exchange" their equipment with that of fallen Union soldiers, to the point where entire brigades were outfitted with Union arms and equipment.

In this manner Confederate soldiers marched and fought for four years against one of the largest and best supplied armies in the world, managing time and again to hold their ground and even win major victories. Joshua Chamberlain, a colonel in the Union army, voiced a common sentiment when he wrote of the Confederate soldiers, "they were the embodiment of manhood; men whom neither toils nor sufferings, nor the fact of death, nor disaster, nor hopelessness could bend from their resolve." The average Confederate soldier, mostly indifferent to the social and economic issues that had led to the South's secession, was fighting for the defense of his homeland against the invading Union armies, and for the right to self-determination, the same cause for which his grandfathers had fought the American Revolution 80 years before.

A Confederate Soldier's Dress and Equipment

Over the course of the 1862 campaigns, the dress and equipment of the Confederate soldier quickly changed from that of the fully equipped, parade-ground soldier, resembling his Northern counterpart in many respects, to the iconic image of the "grey-jacket rebel," one of economy and practicality that lasted to the end of the war. The men threw away anything that weighed them down on long marches, often carrying only a change of underclothes, spare shirt, and socks rolled up in a blanket, along with their musket, ammunition, haversack, and canteen. The uniforms changed too, as men replaced their issue caps with slouch hats, and army depots supplied them with the more economical short jacket and plain, untrimmed clothing.

1. Slouch Hat
2. British Enfield Rifle
3. Frock Jacket
4. Blanket Roll
5. Canteen
6. Haversack
7. Gum Blanket
8. Belt Cartridge Box
9. Bayonet
10. Trousers
11. Bayonet Scabbard

Index

Inkstand 63

J

Jacket 66

K

Knapsack 35
Knife 43

L

Laboratory 25
Letter (correspondence) 51
Lice 55
Lucifers. *See* Matches

M

Mail *See* Letter
Malaria 59
Maple syrup 45
Matches 61
Match safe 61
McCarter, William 46
Mercury fulminate 23
Mess kit 42
Minie Ball 24
Minié, Claude-Étienne 24
Mittens 39, 43
Money 50
Musket 14, 22, 30, 66
Musket tool 30

N

Needle 57
Negative 53
Nettleton, Corporal George 49
Newspaper 48
Nitro-cellulose 52
Nurse 59

O

116th Pennsylvania Infantry 46
121st New York Infantry 58

P

Pan 43
Paper cartridge. *See* Cartridge
Pay 40, 50
Peas 47

Pen 63
Percussion cap 23, 25, 31
Photograph 51, 52
Photographer 52
Photography 51, 52
Physician. *See* Surgeon
Pick 30, 31
Pioneer 37
Pipe (smoking) 60
Plate 42
Playing cards 57
Pork 46
Potato 46

R

Ramrod 32
Razor 55
Reading 48, 70
Recruitment 9
Recruitment poster 3, 10
Regiment 11
Rice 46
Rice, John L. 58
Rifle 14, 22, 30, 66
Rubber blanket. *See* Gum blanket

S

Sack coat 16
Salt pork 46
Scabbard 14, 28, 66
Scissors 57
Scott Archer, Frederick 52
Screwdriver 30
Scruton, Darius K. 8
2nd New Hampshire Infantry 58
17th Maine Regiment 49
Shaving kit 55
Shelter half 36, 41
Shirt 19
Shoes 21
Sibley tent 41
16th Maine Infantry 49
Skillet 43
Slouch hat 66
Smoking 60
Soap 54
Socks 21
Soldier's prayer book 48
Sowbelly. *See* Salt pork
Spoon 43
Springfield rifle 14, 22

Stretcher-bearer 58
Sugar 45
Sumter, fort 8
Surgeon 11, 58
Suspenders 21

T

Tallow 25
Tampion 30
Tent 36, 41
10th New York Regiment 49
3rd New Hampshire Infantry 61
38th Indiana Regiment 46
Tobacco 60
Tobacco twist 60
Toiletries 54
Toothbrush 54
Trousers 21, 66
20th New York Regiment 49
Typhoid 39, 59

W

Waist belt 28
Wallet 50
Waud, Alfred 48
Wentworth, Thomas 9
Wet collodion photography 51
Whitman, Walt 59
Wiper 30
Wrench 30
Writing case 63

FOR FURTHER READING:

Denis Hambucken, Matthew Payson, *Confederate Soldier of the American Civil War.* (Woodstock, Vermont: Countryman Press, 2012)

David W. Blight, ed., *When This Cruel War Is Over: The Civil War Letters of Charles Harvey Brewster* (Northampton: Thomson-Shore Inc., 1992).

Walter Holden, William E. Ross, Elizabeth Slomba, eds., *Stand Firm and Fire Low: The Civil War Writings of Colonel Edward E. Cross* (Hanover, NH: University of New Hampshire Press, 2002).

James Grenier, Janet Coryell, James Smither, eds., *A Surgeon's Civil War: The Letters and Diary of Daniel M. Holt, M.D.* (Kent, Ohio: Kent State University Press, 1994).

James McPherson, *For Cause and Comrades: Why Men Fought in the Civil War* (New York: Oxford University Press, 1997).

Kevin O'Brien, ed., *My Life in the Irish Brigade: The Civil War Memoirs of Private William McCarter, 116th Pennsylvania Infantry* (Cambridge: Da Capo Press, 2003).

Robert Hunt Rhodes ed., *All For The Union: The Civil War Diary and Letters of Elisha Hunt Rhodes* (New York: Orion Books, 1991).

Shelley Swanson Sateren, ed. *A Civil War Drummer Boy: The Diary of William Bircher, 1861–1865* (Mankato, Minnesota: Capstone Press, 2000).

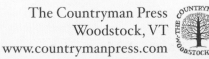

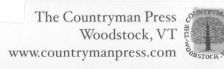